# The Case for a Cultur

CW00820547

Artists for Palestine UK

# Contents

*Foreword* 5
*Introduction* 7

1   Why Israel? 9
2   Palestinian culture denied 13
3   Israel's culture wars: politics by other means 19
4   Not performing in Israel 23
5   Israel abroad: facing the music 27
6   Reasons not to boycott? 33
7   When do I act, and why? 41
8   Moving on 47

*Appendices*
1   What Israel does to the Palestinians 51
2   Who to link up with 55

# Foreword

During my week on the West Bank with the Palestine Festival of Literature in the summer of 2014, I heard the Danish writer Janne Teller talk about the way in which being in Palestine takes all the already-known facts of oppression and apartheid and 'moves them from the brain to the stomach.' I had thought those facts she spoke about were already lodged in my gut courtesy of Palestinian writers such as Raja Shehadeh, Mourid Barghouti and Susan Abulhawa – but being in Palestine teaches you that nothing, not even the most humane and moving books, can make you feel an injustice so deeply as the expression on a young woman's face seconds after an Israeli border guard confiscates her Jerusalem resident permit and she understands she can no longer step foot in the city that is her home, and where her mother is waiting for her to return home from an American college campus.

In my time in Palestine I encountered a spirit of resistance, hope, courage and humanity that was humbling in its power. Why join a cultural boycott? There are many answers to that question laid out with clarity and nuance in this booklet. Of all those answers, here is the one lodged deepest in the gut: because of the Palestinians who are asking it of us. It is not in a spirit of exclusion or bigotry or a misunderstanding of the power of culture that this call for boycott has gone out. It is precisely the opposite.

In a world of too much interventionism here is a chance for internationalism; in a situation that can often seem intractable and in which we feel ourselves powerless, here is a chance to help make a change in a non-violent way.

Kamila Shamsie

# Introduction

When constructive engagement and reasoned argument fail, wrote novelist Iain Banks shortly before his death in 2013, 'the relatively crude weapon of boycott is pretty much all that's left.'

Banks was explaining his decision to deny Israeli publishers the rights to his novels. It was a decision that shocked many – how can one interfere in free cultural exchange for a political objective? And yet a growing number of respected cultural figures align themselves with a boycott movement in support of Palestine.

> *Since the 2010 attack on the Turkish-led convoy to Gaza in international waters, I've instructed my agent not to sell the rights to my novels to Israeli publishers.*[1]
> Iain Banks, author

> *We were asked to play Israel, and we refused. I think the best approach is to boycott a government that seems hell-bent on very destructive policies.*[2]
> Robert del Naja, Massive Attack

> *By inviting Habima [the National Theatre of Israel], Shakespeare's Globe is associating itself with policies of exclusion practised by the Israeli state and endorsed by its national theatre company. We ask the Globe to withdraw the invitation.*[3]
> Emma Thompson, Mark Rylance, Sir Jonathan Miller, David Calder, Dame Harriet Walter and 32 other actors, writers and directors

> *I cannot come, I do not want to come, and I am not coming.*[4]
> Mike Leigh, film director

In 2004, a coalition of Palestinian organisations, PACBI (the Palestinian Campaign for the Academic and Cultural Boycott of Israel), called on 'people of conscience' to 'shoulder the moral responsibility to fight injustice' by boycotting Israel's academic and cultural institutions. The following year this was broadened into a call for general Boycott, Divestment and Sanctions (BDS). The global BDS campaign calls for action against Israel until it fully complies with international law. This means that Israel must:

- Withdraw from all the territory it has occupied since 1967, including East Jerusalem, and remove its illegal settlements.

- Agree to United Nations resolutions on the restitution of the rights of Palestinian refugees.

- Dismantle the system of discriminatory laws and practices that applies within its pre-1967 borders.

The Palestinian call for boycott does not target individual artists according to their nationality, their beliefs, or the content of their art. It focuses on culture's ties to the Israeli state. This booklet analyses what it is about Israel's actions that make boycott both necessary and moral. It looks at the role of culture in Israel's political project and aims to show how cultural boycott can help end Israel's impunity from the law and advance the cause of Palestinian freedom.

For many people cultural boycott goes against the grain. The booklet will address concerns commonly expressed about a cultural boycott of Israel: for example, that it limits freedom of expression, interferes with cultural dialogue, and is even antisemitic in nature.

# 1
# Why Israel?

*There is no other country in the Western world from which the international community has been willing to put up with acts of state violence for five decades, other than Israel.*[5]

Avraham Burg, former speaker of the Knesset
and former chairman of the Jewish Agency

For many years there were two props for Israel's almost automatic support among Western democratic nations and their populations. One was the horror of the Holocaust; the other was the notion that Israel was a small, weak, democratic state, somehow miraculously surviving though surrounded by larger and implacably hostile nations ruled by dictators. This era is over.

The magnitude of the injustices experienced by the Palestinians at the hands of Israel can no longer be denied. The repeated murderous attacks on the besieged Gaza Strip are only the most overt manifestation of these policies. More entrenched are ethnic cleansing, illegal colonisation, racism, torture, imprisonment of children, the denial of statehood. Israeli academic Baruch Kimmerling describes this catalogue of oppression as *politicide*, 'a process that has as its ultimate goal the dissolution of the Palestinian people's existence as a legitimate social, political and economic entity.'[6]

Critics of the boycott will point out that China occupies Tibet and has settled millions of its citizens there; the United States was built on the dispossession and slaughter of Native Americans; Uzbekistan's regime maintains itself through systematic use of barbaric torture; and so on – so why pick on Israel?

The first answer is that in the case of Palestine we have a call for boycott from those who are suffering oppression. PACBI tells us that 'boycotting Israeli academic and cultural institutions is an urgently needed form of pressure against Israel that can bring about its compliance with international law and the requirements for a just peace.' Palestinian civil society has chosen to adopt this non-violent strategy to bring pressure to bear on the powerful and unaccountable.

This use of boycott has numerous successful precedents, notably the decades-long boycott of white-ruled South Africa that was a key contributor to the collapse of apartheid.

## Absence of international sanctions

The second answer is that Israel is sustained by the backing of our own Western governments and many of our businesses and institutions, which gives us both the responsibility and the opportunity to remove this support. There are many countries around the world that face retribution by some or all of the 'international community' for breaching international norms. Israel is not one of them.

At the time of writing, Syria has had its foreign assets frozen, Zimbabwe faces embargoes on international loans and arms imports, and the US and EU have imposed an array of sanctions on Russian individuals and businesses.

But Israel experiences the opposite. It commits war crimes and offends every principle of human rights – and in return it gets rewarded. Since 1948, Israel has received nearly $234bn in US tax dollars.

In February 2014, Amnesty International said Israel had shown 'callous disregard for human life' by shooting and killing dozens of unarmed civilians, including children, in the Occupied Palestinian Territories in the previous three years.[7] In July and August 2014, Israel killed more than two thousand Gazans (of whom only around 276 were members of armed groups), wounded close to 11,000, and reduced the homes of hundreds of thousands to rubble – but US aid continues regardless. The US administration, while bemoaning the scale of civilian deaths, actually re-supplied Israel with ammunition during the 2014 onslaught.

Our governments make Israel's abuses possible. Bilateral trade between Britain and Israel, in the region of £5.1bn in 2013, is reported to be growing. The European Union issued a directive in 2013 preventing any of its funding to Israel being spent on activities in the Occupied Palestinian Territories.[8] But the impact of this restriction is trivial by comparison with that of the wide-ranging EU-Israel Association Agreement, signed in 1995, which remains in place. Israel is *de facto* a member of the EU.

If the diplomatic defence system erected by our own governments[9] had not existed, there would have been UN-backed sanctions on Israel decades ago.

Boycott is a way of dismantling this defence system – of generating pressure on our governments to end the policy of guaranteeing Israel's impunity.

## Why a cultural boycott?

Decades of business-as-usual cultural exchange with Israeli state-supported institutions have not yielded any progress towards rights and justice for the Palestinians, as the besieged people of Gaza can testify. Culture, in the context of Israel's occupation, has not served to 'build bridges', but has acted as a cover for the state's crimes. Cultural import and export are a crucial part of the 'Brand Israel' programme, a strategy aimed at overlaying the brutality of ethnic cleansing and settler colonialism with a veneer of civilised sophistication (this is discussed in more detail in Section 3).

Challenges to this strategy of cultural whitewashing have an important effect. Refusals by British cultural figures like Iain Banks, musicians Elvis Costello and Nigel Kennedy and the physicist and author Stephen Hawking, have generated not only column inches in Israel, but also high-level debates within Israeli intelligence, government and business circles, about how to counter what they see as a serious challenge to the credibility of Israel's narrative abroad. For Israel, culture is never unpolitical.

It is after considerable contemplation that I have lately arrived at the decision that I must withdraw from the two performances scheduled in Israel ...

There are occasions when merely having your name added to a concert schedule may be interpreted as a political act that resonates more than anything that might be sung and it may be assumed that one has no mind for the suffering of the innocent.

I must believe that the audience for the coming concerts would have contained many people who question the policies of their government on settlement and deplore conditions that visit intimidation, humiliation or much worse on Palestinian civilians in the name of national security ...

I hope it is possible to understand that I am not taking this decision lightly or so I may stand beneath any banner, nor is it one in which I imagine myself to possess any unique or eternal truth.

It is a matter of instinct and conscience.[10]

Elvis Costello, musician, May 2010

# 2
## Palestinian culture denied

*Farewell, my library! Farewell, the house of wisdom,*
*the abode of philosophers ... How many sleepless nights*
*I spent there, reading and writing, the night silent,*
*the people asleep ... Goodbye, my books!*[11]

The owner of this library, Khalil Sakakini, pioneering Palestinian educator, free thinker and writer, was one of roughly 750,000 Palestinians that fled or were driven into exile by Israeli forces in 1947/48, and not allowed to return. Sakakini never saw his house or his books again. His library suffered an equally dismal fate: part of it was retained in the National Library of the new Israeli state, catalogued as 'AP' – absentee property – and part of it was pulped.

Israeli researcher Gish Amit, who stumbled on the remaining books of Sakakini and other exiled Palestinians in the National Library, says, 'The ruin of Palestinian culture is the birth moment of a new Israeli consciousness, based not only on erasing the Palestinians' presence, but also on erasing their culture.'[12]

After what Palestinians call 'the catastrophe' of 1948 – the *Nakba* – the new state of Israel set out to 'de-Arabise' the entire landscape. Pine forests and parks were planted over the ruins of many of the 400 or so Palestinian villages that had been forcibly depopulated. David Ben Gurion, first prime minister of Israel, appointed a Governmental Names Commission to re-label each town, village, river and hill. In his words:

*Just as we do not recognise the Arabs' political proprietorship*
*over the country, so also we do not recognise their spiritual*
*proprietorship and their place names.*[13]

Politically-inspired biblical archaeology is still being used today to justify land theft. In East Jerusalem, Palestinian communities are being displaced to make way for a 'City of David' tourist park promoting an exclusive narrative of Jewish origins. The term Israel gives to this still accelerating practice is 'Judaisation'.

## From the 1967 Occupation until now: censorship, sabotage and siege

The suppression of Palestinian culture in the Occupied Territories is still very much on the Israeli agenda. When Israeli forces re-invaded Ramallah in the West Bank in 2002, they ransacked the Sakakini Cultural Centre. The trail of destruction included manuscripts belonging to Palestinian poet Mahmoud Darwish, an Israeli citizen, whose poems were banned from the curricula of schools in Israel until 2012. Darwish said in 2001, 'I just wish they'd read me to enjoy my poetry, not as a representative of the enemy.' The following year, after the Israeli rampage through the Sakakini Cultural Centre, he explained to William Dalrymple:

> *The Israelis wanted to give us a message that nobody and nothing is immune – including our cultural life. I took the message personally. I know they're strong and can invade and kill anyone. But they can't break or occupy my words. That is one thing they can't do. My poetry is the one way I have to resist them.*[14]

Under such conditions, art takes on new layers of political meaning for both occupied and occupier. Before Palestinians in the West Bank can travel to another town to view paintings or hear music, reach a rehearsal of a play or a concert, or tour a performance, they usually require permission from Israel. Randomly – and often – it is withheld.

Cultural exchange, whether among Palestinian artists, between artists and audiences, or between Palestinian and international artists, is anything but free because all Palestinians in the West Bank and Gaza live under siege, their movements conditional on the whim of an Israeli soldier at a checkpoint or an occupation bureaucrat, the practice of their art liable to suppression by a hostile occupation regime.

For example:

- In 2009, the Arab League and UNESCO designated Jerusalem as Capital of Arab Culture for that year. Israel has annexed the whole of Jerusalem, and claims it as the 'eternal capital' of the Jewish state. Israel, therefore, banned all displays of culture connected with 'Al-Quds Capital of Arab Culture' celebrations. Police broke up cultural gatherings in venues across occupied East Jerusalem, arresting twenty festival organisers and participants.[15]

- In June 2012, the Ramallah Orchestra was due to give a concert at St Anne's Church in East Jerusalem, organised with the assistance of the French Consulate. But members of the orchestra living in the West Bank were refused permits to enter occupied East Jerusalem. Instead of the Eroica Symphony, which the orchestra had planned to play, there were enough musicians only for a chamber piece.

- Khamis Abu Shaaban opened the Al-Hashimia bookshop in Gaza in 1942. Seventy one years later, at the age of 91, he told journalists how the importation of books, newspapers and magazines had been almost completely cut off since 2007, following Israel's blockade: 'Throughout all of the decades that I have lived, I have not felt as much pain and sadness as I do during this period … I still come to the bookshop daily and stay until 2pm.'[16]

- Mohammad Bakri, a Palestinian actor who is a citizen of Israel, made *Jenin, Jenin*, a documentary about the Israeli army's invasion of Jenin refugee camp in 2002 and the massacre it committed there. The Israeli Film Ratings Board banned the film; Bakri challenged, and won in the Supreme Court. Then five Israeli soldiers sued him for libel, even though they do not appear in the film; they lost their case on technical grounds. Five years after Bakri completed the film, the military advocate general asked for libel proceedings to be instituted on behalf of the Israel Defence Force. Bakri's employment as an actor continues to be contested by right-wing groups. In 2011, the Hebrew University cut the electricity to the hall where a student group was screening *Jenin, Jenin* with

Bakri present, and summoned the students to appear before a disciplinary board.[17]

These stories barely begin to convey the cruel pettiness that Palestinian artists and musicians under occupation experience – the studios trashed, the violins smashed, the rehearsals missed, the cameras broken, the choirs arrested, the dancers held at checkpoints until the performance is long over.

At least, for now, artists are not being arrested for using the colours of the Palestinian flag in their paintings, as they were during the first *intifada* (or uprising). 'You couldn't paint a poppy', says artist Vera Tamari. 'You'd be imprisoned for painting a watermelon!' Tamari created an installation from the civilian cars crushed by Israeli tanks in Ramallah in 2002:

> *We had a big party to open the exhibit – le tout Ramallah – and went home at midnight. At four that morning, the Israelis invaded again … a whole cohort of Merkavas turned up … and ran over the exhibit, over and over again, backwards and forwards, crushing it to pieces. Then, for good measure, they shelled it. Finally they got out and pissed on the wreckage. I got the whole thing on video, and was delighted – of course. I have always been a great admirer of Duchamp.[18]*

My name is Abdelfattah Abusrour. I am director of Alrowwad cultural and theatre training society, which I founded with a group of friends in 1998 in Aida refugee camp in Bethlehem, Occupied Palestine, where I was born, to create a safe space of beautiful expression, a philosophy that I call beautiful resistance against the ugliness of occupation and its violence ... and to help our children and youth to see their potential as change makers, without needing to carry a gun and shoot everybody else ...

In May 2002, Alrowwad theatre centre was vandalised by the Israeli army. They broke our video cameras and computers, and emptied oil and acrylic painting tubes all over the space. During our tours in the West Bank, many checkpoints forbid us passage with our theatre or dance shows and our play bus. We wait for hours, sometimes without being allowed to pass south to Hebron or to the north. No access is granted to Gaza, to East Jerusalem or 1948 Palestine.

Theatre and arts are about giving a voice to those who are not heard, and defending what we believe is just and right ... That is why for me as an artist, as a theatre practitioner, I boycott every relation with Israeli artists or academics or politicians ... This is not directed against Jews... This boycott is directed against an apartheid system of occupation and discrimination, and all those who are part of it and do not do any action against it. An injustice is an injustice, and an occupation is an occupation, and those who support it, or treat it as normal, are complicit with it.[19]

Abdelfattah Abusrour, Aida Refugee Camp, 2013

# 3
## Israel's culture wars: politics by other means

*We see culture as a propaganda tool of the first rank, and
I do not differentiate between propaganda and culture.*[20]

Nissim Ben-Sheetrit, Israeli foreign ministry, 2005

*It is more important for Israel to be attractive
than to be right.*[21]

Ido Aharoni, Israeli foreign ministry, 2008

*We will send well-known novelists and writers overseas, theatre
companies, exhibits. This way, you show Israel's prettier face,
so we are not thought of purely in the context of war.*[22]

Arye Mekel, Israeli foreign ministry, 2009

In October 2006, the Israeli foreign ministry, the prime minister's office and the finance ministry took over the work of a US group calling itself 'Brand Israel Group', in order to plan 'a comprehensive strategy for the nation's image management.' 'The media always show men with guns,' complained Saar Friedmann, one of many public relations and branding agency people hired along the way.[23]

Re-branding Israel has continued to be a central pre-occupation of the foreign ministry, though successive re-launches have not so far succeeded; 'the dark side of the story won't go away,' says US academic Stephen M. Walt.[24]

A key strategy of the re-branding is to use musicians, filmmakers and other cultural professionals to provide a glittering screen behind which the everyday brutalities of occupation and dispossession are intended to be less visible.

In 2008, Israeli poet Yitzhak Laor published a copy of the contract Israeli artists going abroad with foreign ministry funding were by then required to sign. The contract was between the Israeli artist or company ('the service provider') and the State of Israel, via the foreign ministry's Division for Cultural and Scientific Affairs. Its terms made explicit the promotional requirements attached to government funding for foreign tours:

> *The service provider is aware that the purpose of ordering services from him is to promote the policy interest of the State of Israel via culture and art, including contributing to creating a positive image for Israel.*

And yet this relationship was to remain secret:

> *The service provider will not present himself as an agent, emissary and/or representative of the Ministry.*[25]

Israeli government funding to tour work and promote Israel is a key issue for the boycott movement. Omar Barghouti, a founder of PACBI, told visiting writers in Ramallah in 2013 that the movement had absolutely no problem with artists who derive funding from the state to produce their work in Israel – 'that's your right as a taxpayer', he said. But the movement takes action against companies and artists who accept foreign ministry funding to go abroad – because that, says Barghouti, is 'propaganda'.[26]

## Culture cementing occupation

Culture has a domestic political function. Abroad, it is used to 'sell' a distorted picture of the country and distract from the oppressive reality. But domestically it is deployed, deliberately and self-consciously, as a central part of the project of long-term occupation.

In its illegal settlements in the Occupied Palestinian Territories, Israel builds not only checkpoints and surveillance facilities, but schools, universities and cultural centres.

Take Ariel, an illegal colony on the West Bank, with around 25,000 settlers (and a booming property market). Prime Minister Netanyahu visited Ariel in 2010, and planted a tree to symbolise the permanence of occupation. Later the same year, Ariel's cultural centre was opened, and Israel's two flagship theatre companies, Habima and Cameri, agreed to add it to their touring schedule. Israeli journalist Gideon Levy commented, 'In the heart of an illegal settlement built on a plot of stolen land' the companies put on shows 'to help settlers pass their time pleasantly, while surrounded by people who have been deprived of all their rights'.[27]

The fact that the Cameri Theatre has accepted to support the brutal action of colonisation by playing in Ariel has made us aware that in coming to your theatre we would appear as a support for that brutal action.

This forces us to decline your invitation to perform in your theatre. The decision is entirely ours .. it is our free choice. We know that there are many amongst you and in your country who share our attitude and it is them we wish to support as well as the people of Palestine.[28]

Peter Brook, theatre director, September 2012

# 4
## Not performing in Israel

*I have always had an unwavering belief in art as a unique
arena for public debate. Faced with the political situation
in Israel I have for the first time been forced to ask myself
if silence can sometimes be the strongest message ... When
I choose to cancel the Tel Aviv show, it is because dialogue
has failed. In fact, it has been abused for decades. A discourse
of peace has served as a thick veil, concealing ... the siege
of Gaza, the fragmentation of the West Bank and
the discrimination of Arab-Israeli citizens ... Silence
is the loudest song that I can sing.[29]*

Moddi, musician, January 2014

The acceptance of an invitation to appear in Israel is not politically
neutral. Art is the showcase of sophisticated modern states –
a marker of civilised, progressive and democratic values. Israel
wants to lay claim to these values, and to cram its events and
festivals with foreign artists. Every such visit is publicly celebrated
as a victory against the boycott movement and evidence of moral
support for Israel.

But in the last few years, musicians and actors who announce
their intention to perform in Israel have increasingly had to
engage with activists from across the world who initiate social
media campaigns calling on them to cancel. The American singer
Macy Gray rejected the boycott call, but came to regret her decision;
in 2011 Gray said on Twitter: 'I had a reality check and I stated
that I definitely would not have played there if I had known even
the little that I know now.'[30]

One high-profile online campaign led to the cancellation by
US punk rock artists Jello Biafra and the Guantanamo School
of Medicine of their scheduled performance in 2011. Biafra said:

*I will not perform in Israel unless it is a pro-human
rights, anti-occupation event that does not violate the spirit
of the boycott.[31]*

# Literary awards industry

Israel has many literary festivals and its establishment is keen to invite foreign writers, regularly awarding them generous prizes. These are writers who in several cases have strong liberal credentials, and their presence is particularly advantageous for a country whose record of oppression is under a permanent spotlight.

British writer Ian McEwan, who accepted the Jerusalem Prize in 2011, said 'I think one should always make a distinction between a civil society and its government. It is the Jerusalem book fair, not the Israeli foreign ministry, which is making the award. I would urge people to make the distinction – it is about literature.'[32]

But in Israel, most of the bodies that award literary prizes don't stand apart from politics – they are complicit in Israeli government policy. When McEwan went to Israel to collect his prize, he was first photographed joining the weekly protest in the Jerusalem neighbourhood of Sheikh Jarrah, where Palestinian families are being expelled to make way for Israeli settlers. But he went on to receive his prize from, and shake hands with, the authors of the very policies he protested, openly racist Jerusalem mayor Nir Barkat and then-president of Israel, Shimon Peres.

Israeli campaign groups Boycott from Within and Sheikh Jarrah Solidarity protested McEwan's actions. Their statement read:

> *Distinguished scholars such as Judith Butler and Naomi Klein have visited Sheikh Jarrah and other parts of Israel's backyard without legitimizing those responsible for the crimes of apartheid and occupation committed there. By accepting the Jerusalem Prize, McEwan has allowed the perpetrators of these crimes, such as Nir Barkat, to ... disseminate the blatant lie that 'we promote tolerance here in Jerusalem, an open city'.*

In May 2010, Amitav Ghosh and Margaret Atwood accepted the $1 million Dan David prize from Israeli president Shimon Peres, in spite of many appeals to them not to do so.[33] Ghosh wrote, 'This prize is awarded by a university in conjunction with a private foundation: it is not awarded by the state of Israel.'

But Tel Aviv University (TAU), where the Dan David Foundation is based, is built on the ruins of the Palestinian village of Shaikh Muwannis, destroyed in 1948. The university celebrates its relationship with the Israel Defence Forces. The TAU Review for 2008-9 trumpeted the 50 funded projects it had for the military and the defence industry. Its then president Zvi Galil said, 'I myself am awed by the magnitude and scientific creativity of the work being done behind the scenes at TAU that enhances the country's … military edge.' In July 2014, with slaughter and destruction gathering pace in Gaza, the TAU administration sent a letter to staff saying TAU 'embraces and strengthens the hands of the security forces', and threatening disciplinary action against staff and students voicing criticism on social media.[34]

**I was just invited to Israel as a guest of honour at the Haifa International Film Festival. I will not be going to Israel at this time. I will go to Israel when the walls come down. I will go to Israel when occupation is gone. I will go to Israel when the state does not privilege one religion over another. I will go to Israel when Apartheid is over.[35]**

Mira Nair, film director, July 2013

We support the Palestinian struggle for freedom, justice and equality. In response to the call from Palestinian artists and cultural workers for a cultural boycott of Israel, we pledge to accept neither professional invitations to Israel, nor funding, from any institutions linked to its government until it complies with international law and universal principles of human rights.

This pledge was initiated in 2014, by and for people working in the arts in Britain. At the time of publication of this booklet, it had been signed by 700 artists and cultural workers. Further signatures can be added at www.artistsforpalestine.org.uk

# 5

# Israel abroad: facing the music

*I do not believe that a State that maintains an occupation,
committing on a daily basis crimes against civilians, deserves
to be invited to any kind of cultural event. That is, it
is anti-cultural; it is a barbarian act masked as culture in
the most cynical way. It manifests support for Israel, and ...
sustains the occupation.*[36]

Aharon Shabtai, Israeli poet, February 2008

The scale and intensity of the Brand Israel project have made
its high profile cultural ambassadors targets for political protest.
Each challenge to the presentation of Israel as a country entitled
to 'business as usual' with the rest of the world has generated
a wealth of argument and debate among performers, commentators
and public. Our examples focus on events in the United Kingdom,
but such actions take place all around the world, vigorous responses
to a version of culture in which the choreographer and the politician,
the conductor's baton and the soldier's rifle, are rarely far apart.

## Dance

Israeli dance company Batsheva was picketed by large numbers
of demonstrators during the Edinburgh International Festival
in 2012. In an interview with a Canadian newspaper in 2005, its
artistic director Ohad Naharin had agreed that war crimes *were*
being committed just 20 kilometres from where he created his
work. He went on to tell demonstrators it was true that 'Batsheva
is here representing Israel'. But, he argued, his company represented
a different Israel, one that should be embraced by friends of the
Palestinians.[37]

However, Batsheva receives funding from the Ministry of Foreign
Affairs for its international tours. Indeed Israeli culture minister
Limor Livnat travelled to Edinburgh to attend the opening night
with the Israeli ambassador to the UK. The *Jewish Telegraph* quoted

Livnat as celebrating Batsheva as 'one of our flagship cultural institutions.'[38] Representation of the Israeli state at Batsheva's performances made it clear that the visit had more than cultural significance. There were nightly protests at its shows in a campaign that won support from many people from the world of arts, among them Liz Lochhead, Scotland's *makar* (or national poet), who had recently visited the Occupied Territories.

## Classical music

In the 1970s, performances of the Red Army Choir and the Bolshoi Ballet in London were disrupted by people campaigning on behalf of Soviet Jews. These activists had no difficulty crossing the supposed line between culture and politics that opponents of the Israeli boycott now defend so fiercely. It was different when BDS supporters sang a rewritten version of Beethoven's *Ode to Joy* during a Prom concert by the Israel Philharmonic Orchestra (IPO) in London in September 2011, and shouted slogans before the second half began. The BBC took the live transmission off-air – for the first time in the 75-year history of the Proms.[39] This unintended amplification of the BDS action inside the concert hall generated a worldwide storm of publicity and of polemical comment.

BDS activists were not targeting Israeli music; they were drawing attention to the links between the IPO and the Israeli state. For the IPO's history is entwined with that of Israeli conquest, celebrating army triumphs, from the seizure of Beersheva in 1949 to the capture of Jerusalem in 1967.

At the time of the protests, the orchestra's 'About Us' page boasted of its 'special concerts for IDF soldiers' at what it called 'their outposts' – in the illegal settlements. The IPO has, says its conductor Zubin Mehta, often 'served as an ambassador for Israel'.[40]

# A national theatre

In 2012, fresh from its performances in the settlement town of Ariel, Habima, Israel's national theatre company, was invited to take part in the London Globe to Globe festival. In addition to its usual government subsidy, Habima had funding from the foreign ministry to cover a £10,000 shortfall in finances for its London trip. Indeed the ardently pro-Israel *Jewish Chronicle* quoted an Embassy spokesman saying 'that the Foreign Ministry was the "biggest exporter of Israeli culture to the world" and would ensure that the performance went ahead.'[41]

Many actors, writers and directors working in the UK protested against this invitation.

*We notice with dismay and regret that Shakespeare's Globe Theatre in London has invited Israel's National Theatre, Habima, to perform The Merchant of Venice in its Globe to Globe festival this coming May. The general manager of Habima has declared the invitation 'an honourable accomplishment for the State of Israel'. But Habima has a shameful record of involvement with illegal Israeli settlements in Occupied Palestinian Territory. Last year, two large Israeli settlements established 'halls of culture' and asked Israeli theatre groups to perform there. A number of Israeli theatre professionals – actors, stage directors, playwrights – declared they would not take part.*

*Habima, however, accepted the invitation with alacrity, and promised the Israeli minister of culture that it would 'deal with any problems hindering such performances'. By inviting Habima, Shakespeare's Globe is undermining the conscientious Israeli actors and playwrights who have refused to break international law.*

*The Globe says it wants to 'include' the Hebrew language in its festival – we have no problem with that. 'Inclusiveness' is a core value of arts policy in Britain, and we support it.*

> *But by inviting Habima, the Globe is associating itself with policies of exclusion practised by the Israeli state and endorsed by its national theatre company. We ask the Globe to withdraw the invitation so that the festival is not complicit with human rights violations and the illegal colonisation of occupied land.* [42]
>
> Signed by: Emma Thompson, Mark Rylance, Sir Jonathan Miller, David Calder, Dame Harriet Walter and 32 other theatre professionals, letter to the *Guardian*, 29 March 2012

The resulting public debate put the question of Palestine squarely in front of audiences and a wider public. Ashtar, the Palestinian company which also performed at the festival, organised a packed-out meeting, where its actors talked of rehearsals made near-impossible by checkpoints and pass laws, and actors strip-searched on their way to perform in London. 'At night Israeli artists want to perform with us,' said Ashtar's director Iman Aoun, 'and in the morning they serve in the army.'

Protest against Habima did not close down dialogue, as some critics have argued. Instead it opened people's eyes both to the suppression of Palestinian culture and to Israeli attempts to use culture as a smokescreen to conceal oppression. This was one episode in a growing campaign: boycott in general, and cultural boycott in particular, have generated proliferating debates around the world about Israel's multiple violations of Palestinian rights. Boycott serves to puncture the wall of silence and denial which for too long has enabled Israel to escape the full censure its policies deserve.

## A local theatre

In July 2014, the Tricycle Theatre in Kilburn was preparing, for the 8th time, to host the annual UK Jewish Film Festival, which is partly funded by the Israeli Embassy. July also saw the beginning of Operation Protective Edge, the Israeli onslaught on Gaza which killed more than 2,000 Palestinians.

In the midst of massive protests against Israel, Jonathan Levy, Chairman of the theatre board, informed the organisers of the Film Festival that they could not host this year's festival unless the UKJFF severed its funding ties with the Israeli embassy. The theatre offered to provide alternative funding to cover the loss of the contribution [£1,400] from the embassy. The Jewish Film Festival walked away from the Tricycle, and announced to the press that an 'inherently apolitical' event was being 'boycotted'. The Tricycle issued a statement in response to 'misleading information', clarifying that 'at this moment, the Tricycle would not accept sponsorship from any government agency involved in the conflict.' The Tricycle's statement was cautiously worded but its significance was clear: a high-profile theatre was distancing itself from Brand Israel. Newspaper columnists – especially in the *Guardian* – queued up to claim that the festival had been 'banned' and was the victim of antisemitism. While Gaza was being bombed to rubble, pro-Israel demonstrators appeared outside the theatre. Campaigns were launched to persuade donors to withdraw funding. Sajid Javid, culture secretary in the British government, allowed himself to be quoted saying the theatre was 'misguided' – and it is on his department, via the Arts Council, that the Tricycle is dependent for the bulk of its funding. Javid is on record as regarding Israel as a land that offers the 'warm embrace of freedom and liberty'.[43]

Facing pressure on many fronts, the Tricycle withdrew its opposition to the embassy funds. The power of intimidation, as much behind closed doors as out in the open, was clear. Yet theatre workers rallied to the support of the Tricycle – 500 signed a letter to the *Guardian*: 'Punishing a small theatre for standing up for its principles,' they said, 'is a big step backwards for anyone concerned with challenging prejudice or promoting freedom of speech.'[44]

Shortly after the Tricycle was bullied into submission, *Encounters*, the Bristol film festival, refused Israeli embassy funding.[45] The powers of Britain's own Israel lobby should not be underestimated. But neither should the resilience of our arts community.

I can't say which incident in that crowded nine days turned me into someone who feels that we must use all possible means, all the time, always, of bringing the attention of our world to the Israeli apartheid, for that is what it is - to the appalling and illegal actions of Israel. The Wall. The settlements …

Was it 'a wee thing' like the arrogance of the soldier demanding the passports at Kalandia Checkpoint; or the heart-breaking testimony of the man in the tent in the desert with his thin sheep and scrawny goats in the burning stones of the Jordan Valley who had endured two house demolitions, rebuilt and resisted, and resisted - but was giving up and moving to the ghetto of the nearby 'city' because the Israelis were disrupting the service of the school bus every other day, and he just couldn't bear to see his children deprived of an education?

Or … was it the bullet-holes in the lintels of The House of Poetry in Ramallah?

We must use all means. Including protesting at a dance company. Including total cultural and academic boycott.[46]

Liz Lochhead, Scots national poet, September 2012

# 6
## Reasons not to boycott?

Understandably, many people have doubts about joining in the cultural boycott of Israel, either because it is a 'cultural' boycott, or because of its focus on Israel. In this section, we try to state each objection as persuasively as possible, and give the best answer we can.

## Isn't boycott in general, and cultural boycott in particular, just antisemitism in action?

What critics of boycott say:

> *Antisemitism, a very specific form of racism, is a centuries-old phenomenon deeply embedded in western societies. Doesn't the movement to boycott Israel provide an ideal and apparently legitimate channel for both underground and explicit antisemitism to find expression?*

The Palestinian organisations whose call for boycott motivated the cultural boycott campaign, PACBI and the Boycott National Committee, are both explicitly anti-racist, clear that Jewish people do not stand proxy for the Israeli state, whatever many Zionist leaders may assert. Omar Barghouti, a leading figure in PACBI, put it this way in his address to the Palestine Solidarity Campaign's Annual General Meeting in London in 2012:

> *BDS is a universalist movement that categorically opposes all forms of racism, including Islamophobia and anti-Semitism. This is not negotiable. We should never welcome racists in our midst, no matter what.*[47]

The clear intention of allegations of antisemitism is to deflect criticism of Israel, to intimidate critics and to silence serious debate. As just one instance among many, consider the case of the distinguished British scholar of antisemitism, Oxford academic Brian Klug. He was invited to give the keynote address in November 2013 at Berlin's Jewish Museum, at a conference on antisemitism in Europe today.

A dossier with 17 individual contributions was launched, with maximum publicity, in a bid to strong-arm the museum into dis-inviting him. Klug's crime? To analyse and authoritatively undermine the charge that criticism of Israel equals antisemitism.[48]

There are a very significant number of active Jewish members in all the pro-boycott organisations in the UK and other countries. Membership by Jews of such organisations is sufficient to have the label of 'self-hating Jews' pinned on them by those who wish to discount their views.

There is a danger that fears of being thought an antisemite can deter genuine defenders of Palestinian rights, even when they understand the efficacy and legitimacy of boycott as a tactic. A Jewish supporter of the boycott set out to allay such fears during one controversial campaign, writing: 'Human rights abuses do not become excusable because committed by Jews. The very idea smacks of a kind of twisted, reverse antisemitism.'[49]

## What about the Holocaust?

What critics of boycott say:

> *Surely we shouldn't forget the special circumstances of the Holocaust, which demonstrated to the whole world the need for a state where Jewish people would be safe.*

Nothing in a people's past – not even the horrors of the Holocaust – can be used to justify or excuse crimes against another people. Furthermore, many Jews reject the Zionist argument that Jewish salvation lies in separation from the rest of humanity. They do not believe that Jews in Israel are safer than those elsewhere, or that Jews in the world are safer because of the existence of an exclusivist Jewish state in permanent enmity with its Arab neighbours in the

Middle East. On the contrary, the attempt to drown out the cogent arguments of the boycott movement with cries of 'Holocaust' and 'antisemite', by implicating all Jews in Israel's crimes, stokes hostility against them.

## Given their own relationship to the British state, are cultural workers in this country in any position to make demands on their Israeli counterparts?

What critics of boycott say:

> *Cultural workers in the UK who are calling for boycott accept funding from their own state, which invaded Iraq (for instance). Yet they tell cultural festivals in Britain that unless they reject grants from the Israeli embassy, they will face boycott. This is a clear case of double standards.*

Boycotts are selective, but this does not mean that they are morally tarnished. When the world responded (slowly at first) to the call to boycott apartheid South Africa, it was, in one sense, applying a double standard. It boycotted the South African regime, but not the USA, which was engaged at the time in violent secret wars in Latin America, Africa and Asia. Was it hypocritical for an artist who refused to perform in the Bantustan enclave of Sun City to play in Las Vegas? Only if one takes an entirely abstract view of ethics.

In South Africa, a movement of the oppressed was appealing to the world to take action to isolate and weaken the oppressor. How could an artist turn down that appeal on the grounds that the rand and the dollar were equally blood-stained currencies?

If the demands of 'consistency' lead to the claim that nothing can be done unless and until everything is done, then passivity is bound to be the result. This, in relation to Israel, is surely what the critics intend.

# Isn't Israel quite different from South Africa?

What critics of boycott say:

*Everyone agrees that the boycott of South Africa was morally justified, but Israel isn't South Africa. It doesn't have apartheid. Palestinians in Israel have a vote, and some even hold high office.*

People draw parallels between Israel and South Africa because of this common feature: the existence of a dominant group, defined along racial lines, that monopolises effective power and maintains it through a network of administrative controls backed up by racially-oriented legislation and brutal enforcement. In 1973 the International Convention on the Suppression and Punishment of the Crime of Apartheid (ICSPCA) was adopted by the United Nations General Assembly. ICSPCA defines the crime of apartheid as 'inhuman acts committed for the purpose of establishing and maintaining domination by one racial group ... over another racial group ... and systematically oppressing them'. More than 30 years later, the UN Special Rapporteur on human rights in the Occupied Palestinian Territories, Professor John Dugard (himself a South African), concluded that 'elements of the Israeli occupation constitute forms of colonialism and of apartheid, which are contrary to international law'.[50]

In Israel, there are colour-coded identity documents and vehicle registration plates, settler-only roads, checkpoints, aerial drone surveillance and of course the apartheid Wall – all of which make it easy to identify a person in the wrong place. Town planning controls are deployed to keep Jewish areas free of Palestinians, or to dislodge them from areas of intended Jewish expansion. Schools in Palestinian areas are kept starved of funds to ensure a sub-standard education, and the curricula prevent children from learning about their own history and cultural heritage. The settler-only roads divide the Palestinian West Bank into overcrowded and impoverished bantustans.

There are differences, of course: one is that the basic Israeli imperative has always been quite distinct from apartheid South

Africa's – Israel wants to get rid of Palestinians, whereas the South African apartheid regime wanted to keep black people for their labour.

## Won't a boycott just harden Israeli attitudes?

What critics of boycott say:

> *Even if boycott proves ineffective, it is still likely to be taken by Israelis as evidence of world hostility, with an antisemitic undertow. The probable outcome will be a still more aggressive stance on peace negotiations, and towards the Palestinians.*

There is no doubt that successive Israeli governments have moved (even) further to the right. However, at least until recently, polls showed a substantial majority of ordinary Israelis favouring a negotiated settlement with the Palestinians, even though doubting that it would be achieved. The problem is that to achieve peace would require Israelis to make significant material concessions and, at present, Israelis would rather keep the status quo than make the sacrifices (of land, of control, of identity) needed to come to terms with Palestinians and their reasonable aspirations.

The solution has to be for Israelis to realise that actions have consequences. Boycott alone will not achieve that. Boycott is a step on a path which will in turn take in the withdrawal of investments, the cessation of new investment funds, and the imposition of trade and other sanctions by nations and by international bodies. Each step prepares the way for the next. Intermediate steps may produce a hardening of attitudes. That is what happened with apartheid South Africa, but in the end the inability to borrow on international financial markets and the increasing isolation of white South Africa brought even the intransigent Afrikaners to the negotiating table. Israelis and their governments need the same incentives.

# Why antagonise Israel's cultural workers?

What critics of boycott say:

*Israel's cultural workers are more sympathetic to Palestinian rights than most Israelis. Their work often challenges the status quo. Why antagonise them with a boycott?*

There are forthright supporters of Palestinian rights, including the right to self-determination, among Israeli cultural workers, as indeed there are in many sectors of Israel's population. They are regrettably few, however, and those who actively support Palestinian rights are isolated figures within their peer groups. Liberal Zionists may bemoan the occupation, but only in order to preserve the Jewish state and fend off the threat of being forced into sharing one state equally with Palestinians. Consider the well-known and distinguished liberal authors David Grossman, Amos Oz and AB Yehoshua. In earlier incarnations they were prominent figures in the Israeli peace movement. By 2008 they were supporters of the Cast Lead assault on Gaza in which more than 1,400 died, including hundreds of children.

Even so, it is important to point out that the cultural boycott is not directed against individuals. It is institutional, aimed at bodies that receive Israeli state funding for international visits and tours. None of the major Israeli arts institutions have so far aligned themselves publicly with the suffering of the Palestinians. In a situation as extreme as that of Israel, with death, dispossession and humiliation being dispensed just a few minutes' drive from Israeli artists' own front doors, public silence is complicity.

## Instead of boycott, why not concentrate on supporting Palestinians artists?

What critics of boycott say:

*Boycott is so negative. Why not concentrate on positive support for Palestinian artists, and encourage other artists to go and see the situation for themselves?*

These are not two competing alternatives. The arguments for cultural boycott are, we believe, cogent. And nothing in the cultural boycott of Israel conflicts with supporting Palestinian culture.

Boycott offers a field of action to people who might not have the resources to make a difference to Palestinian art and culture. Some UK cultural workers who support boycott will be able to use their positions and networks to help make things happen. We must hope they will make opportunities to support Palestinian artistic creativity, which, considering the context in which it operates, shows remarkable vibrancy. Artists who visit the Occupied Palestinian Territories are likely to receive the warmest of welcomes, as well as getting an education in what living under occupation actually means.

# 7

## When do I act, and why?

Everyone has a stake in culture and in human rights, and can play a role in boycott. But if you support the Palestinian call for cultural boycott in principle, what does this mean in practice?

Crucially, *this boycott does not target independent artists according to their nationality, their beliefs, or the content of their art.* Instead it focuses on culture's ties to the Israeli state, and, unlike the blanket boycott of apartheid South Africa, is directed at 'official' culture and at institutions that are linked with Israel's regime.

PACBI have formalised guidelines[51] which are helpful in avoiding pitfalls and inconsistencies of practice. These guidelines advise that locally-based movements, knowing their own social and political contexts, need to make their own judgements as to what boycott activities will gather support. And inevitably many cultural events and projects fall in grey areas which require the exercise of judgement. The PACBI guidelines help us to navigate more confidently. If you are still in doubt after reading them, consult PACBI for their advice or talk to colleagues involved in one of the campaign groups listed in the appendix.

The following are some of the principal decisions cultural workers, audiences and campaigners face when it comes to Israel. The questions and answers apply across all branches of cultural production.

## Not performing or exhibiting in Israel

## What should my answer be if I am asked to perform or exhibit in Israel?

There is a simple answer: refuse the invitation. If you have already agreed, withdraw. Your boycott will be much more effective if you give the reasons for your decision.

## Isn't it OK to perform or exhibit in Israel - surely it's only the settlements that are being boycotted?

Absolutely not. The boycott applies to all Israeli institutions. The integration of pre-1967 Israel and the Occupied Palestinian Territories has been an ongoing project for approaching 50 years. Almost all Israeli institutions are complicit, either directly or through their silence.

## But what if the organiser of my trip suggests I can also show my work in the Occupied Territories?

The answer is the same. This would be a form of normalisation – in effect saying the occupation is OK so long as we can perform for Palestinians. For this reason most Palestinian arts organisations will want nothing to do with someone who performs in Israel.

## What if my film is invited to participate in an Israeli film festival, my paintings in an exhibition, or my book in a literary festival?

Wherever you have control over the circulation or distribution of your work, you are urged to refuse the invitation.

## What if I have been invited to Israel to receive a prize, accept a commission, or participate in a residency?

All of these activities will involve an Israeli institution that is subject to boycott because of its ties to the state, its silence about the crimes against human rights, law and dignity taking place on its front doorstep, or its active involvement in justifying, whitewashing or deliberately diverting attention from Israel's violations.

# Are there any circumstances in which I can go to Israel as an artist?

Yes – if the purpose of your visit is to work with individuals or organisations which explicitly oppose the occupation and all the other associated policies.

Dear ...,

Thank you very much for your kind invitation. In other circumstances I would be very happy to visit and participate in your festival. However, I am very sorry to tell you that I am unable to accept your invitation.

For some years I have been an active supporter of the campaign for the academic and cultural boycott of Israel and have decided not to visit Israel or show my work in state-funded Israeli institutions at this time. This was not an easy decision for me as I am an internationalist who believes strongly in the benefits of cultural exchange, not least with my Israeli colleagues. However, after the 'Operation Cast Lead' attacks on Gaza I decided that I would support the Palestinian call for boycott and refuse to visit Israel until its government showed some real willingness to respect international law, stop the expansion of settlements, end the occupation and the blockade of Gaza and honour the human rights of the Palestinian people, including those living within Israel itself.

I sincerely hope that you will understand my position. I feel honoured by your invitation and am very sad that I cannot accept it. I hope to visit Israel again in happier times. [52]

John Smith, artist filmmaker, March 2014

# Boycotting Israel in Britain

## An independent Israeli artist is having her work shown in a UK gallery - should the exhibition be boycotted?

No. This is an *institutional* boycott. (But there could be an issue about the sponsorship of the event – see below on funding.)

## A UK festival has received sponsorship from the Israeli Embassy or other complicit source (see below). What should be done?

Call for the money to be returned. If you are a participating artist, consider withdrawing.

## An Israeli cultural festival is advertised to take place in the UK. Should it be targeted?

The question of funding (see below) is crucial. If the event is receiving Israeli state-sourced funding, the host organisation or venue should be persuaded to give it back. This has succeeded in the past.

## An Israeli orchestra or a major dance or theatre company is due to perform in the UK. Should we campaign against this visit?

The question of funding (see below) is crucial, but for established cultural organisations the answer is almost certainly 'yes'. One reason is that almost all significant Israeli cultural institutions are proud to serve as cultural ambassadors for Israel, to perform in the settlements or give special concerts for the military. Official Israeli cultural exports receive specific state funding for their international work from the Ministry of Foreign Affairs, so the visiting company, host organisation or venue can be asked whether they will reject that funding.

## When is an independent artist no longer independent?

No independent artist should be targeted for boycott. The funding an Israeli artist receives through regular state funding mechanisms for the arts (as opposed to the Ministry of Foreign Affairs, for example), or as part of their employment, does not attract boycott.

However, individual artists are boycottable if their international appearance is sponsored by the Ministry of Foreign Affairs, they formally represent an Israeli cultural institution, or are presented as cultural ambassadors for Israel.

## What constitutes Israeli sourced funding?

Sponsorship of Israeli cultural exports may be provided by an Israeli government ministry or agency, by the Israeli embassy, by BIARTS (a joint Israeli and British government scheme to cement cultural links) or by Israel advocacy and public relations institutions in the UK, such as BICOM (the British Israel Communications & Research Centre). All of the above make the event they support subject to boycott.

# 8
## Moving on

Israel defies international law, suppresses the human rights of Palestinians, attempts to obliterate Palestinian culture and national identity. This outrageous campaign is aimed at taking a land which belongs to others. Nothing in one people's past can justify inflicting this treatment on another.

The Western democracies praise, support and prop up Israel, and protect it from the consequences of its actions, not least at the United Nations. We need to give them a wake-up call. Boycott is a practical means of harnessing the power of the grassroots to be an effective motor for change.

Brand Israel activities funded by the Israeli government are increasingly being challenged in many countries. Just as with South Africa, trades unions and student unions are coming out for boycott, and are changing the political climate. Withdrawals by artists scheduled to visit Israel are increasing in number. Many performers now refuse to include Israel on their schedules.

Because of art's power to move and to influence people, those who work in the cultural field have a particular responsibility to speak out when art and platforms for cultural exchange are used to mask injustice. Action by cultural workers can bring home the need to end the denial of Palestinian rights, aspirations and cultural identity – and the complicity of our governments in that denial.

Cultural boycott is a vibrant international movement. Breaking the boycott must come to be seen as both unprincipled and short-sighted.

Cultural boycott will continue and grow until Palestinians regain their full rights including self-determination. Our job is to bring that day forward.

# Appendices

## 1
## What Israel does to the Palestinians

For those who don't already know what Israel's policies mean on the ground, it is almost impossible to imagine the thoroughness and detail with which they permeate every aspect of Palestinian life. Palestinians describe this system as the combination of settler colonialism, ethnic cleansing and apartheid.

What follows offers a few snapshots of the Palestinian experience.

## Discrimination against Palestinians in Israel

A common claim in defence of Israel is that it is 'at least' a democracy, unlike, say, China. But the 1.3 million Palestinians who live in Israel, who have Israeli citizenship and vote in elections, are nonetheless subject to an array of systematically discriminatory laws and practices which would be illegal in Britain. Adalah, the Legal Centre for Arab Minority Rights in Israel, lists 'more than 50 Israeli laws that discriminate against Palestinian citizens of Israel in all areas of life, including their rights to political participation, access to land, education, state budget resources, and criminal procedures'.[53]

One law that has a devastating impact is the Citizenship and Entry into Israel Law of 2003. It severely restricts Palestinian Arab citizens of Israel from living together in Israel with their Palestinian spouses from the Occupied Palestinian Territories or from 'enemy states', defined by the law as Syria, Lebanon, Iran and Iraq. In Adalah's view: 'The Supreme Court approved a law the likes of which do not exist in any democratic state in the world, depriving citizens from maintaining a family life in Israel only on the basis of the ethnicity or national belonging of their spouse.' At the time of writing, Adalah reported 29 additional discriminatory bills passing through the Knesset system.

# Ethnic cleansing and the Greater Israel project

*That has to be clear. It is impossible to evade it. Without the uprooting of the Palestinians [726,000 of them], a Jewish state would not have arisen here.*[54]

Benny Morris, Israeli historian, 2004

Since before the establishment of Israel, the aim has been to secure as much territory for the state with as few Palestinians in it as possible. The deliberate ethnic cleansing of 1947-8 displaced the majority of Palestinians to neighbouring states. Those forced out, and their descendants, are denied the right to return, and live in exile. Two out of every five of the world's refugees are Palestinian.

In stark contrast, anyone who can claim Jewish descent, wherever they live in the world and regardless of whether or not they have any family connection with the land, has an automatic entitlement to all the privileges of Israeli citizenship.

After 1967, the situation of Palestinians deteriorated further: the war brought millions of them in the West Bank and Gaza under Israeli control. The refugee camps also became bigger and more numerous. Between Israel's illegal and de-facto annexation of Jerusalem in 1967 and 2010, over 14,000 Jerusalem IDs were revoked, forcing Palestinians to either leave the city or reside within it illegally.[55] The ID-based exclusion prevents many Palestinians from accessing their own homes, leaving them liable to confiscation.

The 'Arab demographic danger' has been stressed by Israeli academic geographers and military people alike. Many Israeli policies can be understood as aiming to make life for Palestinians so unpleasant that they will leave. The 'separation wall' became an opportunity to secure 8.5 per cent of West Bank land onto the Israeli side, but without its Palestinian farming owners. Building controls, planning regulations and legalistic pretexts are used to prevent Palestinians from building the homes they need, and to demolish those that they have in areas eyed for Jewish encroachment. Together with the burgeoning settlements and the apartheid road system, all this forces Palestinians into overcrowded and impoverished bantustans. Other results include the disruption of social relations and of education, and indeed the devastation of the local economy.

In the Gaza Strip, 1.8 million Palestinians live within what is in effect an open-air prison, subject to periodic attack by Israel. The occupying state's actions there constitute an unlawful collective punishment of the Palestinian people. Israel's Cast Lead assault on Gaza in December 2008/January 2009 killed some 1,400 Palestinians, the great majority non-combatants by any standards, and injured another 5,000. Twenty thousand people were made homeless. Protective Edge in 2014 was even more savage. The Goldstone Report[56] on Cast Lead for the United Nations found that there was a prima facie case that the IDF (as well as Palestinian militant groups) had committed war crimes and possibly crimes against humanity.

## Impunity

The day after the Cast Lead attacks ended, presidents and prime ministers from Britain, Italy, Germany, France, Spain and the Czech Republic attended a gala dinner in Jerusalem hosted by Israeli Prime Minister Ehud Olmert. As an Israeli official boasted to the *Jerusalem Post*, 'Six world leaders dropped everything to come here and express their support for Israel's security.'[57]

The European Union signed an Association Agreement with Israel in 1995, which has been progressively developed over time. This gives Israel virtually all the benefits of actual membership – access to markets, membership of key committees, participation in research funding sources.

> *Israel, allow me to say, is a member of the European Union without being a member of the institutions. It's a member of all the programmes, it participates in all the programmes.*[58]
> Xavier Solano, EU foreign policy chief, 2009

In effect Israel *is* a member of the EU, while flagrantly violating the common values and human rights commitments that are supposed to bind EU member states together. In the international arena the US watches Israel's back. Between 1967 and 2011, the US vetoed 42 UN Security Council resolutions critical of Israel. Often the US was almost alone in its negative vote. Indeed, of the 55 single-handed vetoes that the US has exercised at the UN, only 15 were *not* in support of Israel.[59]

# 2
## Who to link up with

There are now many sources of information about cultural boycott. There is a comprehensive list on the PACBI website, and a selection of these are listed below.

## Palestine

- Palestinian Campaign for the Academic & Cultural Boycott of Israel (PACBI) - www.pacbi.org
- Palestinian BDS National Committee - www.bdsmovement.net

## UK

- Artists for Palestine UK - www.artistsforpalestine.org.uk
- Boycott Israel Network - www.boycottisraelnetwork.net
- British Committee for the Universities of Palestine - www.bricup.org.uk
- British Writers in Support of Palestine - www.bwisp.wordpress.com
- Architects and Planners for Justice in Palestine - www.apjp.org
- Jews for Boycotting Israeli Goods - www.jews4big.wordpress.com
- Palestine Solidarity Campaign - www.palestinecampaign.org
- Scottish Palestine Solidarity Campaign - www.scottishpsc.org.uk

## Other

- Boycott from Within (Israel) - www.boycottisrael.info
- BDS South Africa - www.bdssouthafrica.com
- US Campaign for the Academic and Cultural Boycott of Israel - www.usacbi.wordpress.com
- Indian Campaign for the Academic and Cultural Boycott of Israel - www.incacbi.in
- Ireland Palestine Solidarity Campaign - www.ipsc.ie
- Refrain Playing Israel - www.refrainplayingisrael.blogspot.com

# 3
# Notes

1. Iain Banks, *Why I'm supporting a cultural boycott of Israel*, Guardian, 5 April 2013

2. William Parry, *The silent treatment*, New Statesman, 3 September 2010

3. *Dismay at Globe invitation to Israeli theatre*, Guardian, 29 March 2012

4. *Mike Leigh cancels Israel trip over loyalty oath*, posted on 18 October 2010 at www.bbc.co.uk/news/entertainment-arts-11566956

5. Avraham Burg, *When the walls come tumbling down*, Haaretz, 1 April 2011

6. Baruch Kimmerling, *Politicide: Ariel Sharon's War Against the Palestinians*, Foreign Affairs, November/December 2003

7. *Israel and Occupied Palestinian Territories: Trigger-Happy: Israel's Use of Excessive Force in the West Bank*, Amnesty International, 27 February 2014

8. Harriet Sherwood, *EU takes tougher stance on Israeli settlements*, Guardian, 16 July 2013

9. A historical account of the political, economic and ideological reasons for the West's unconditional support for Israel can be found in a wide range of literature, including Edward Said, *The Question of Palestine*, Vintage Books, 1992, and Noam Chomsky, *The Fateful Triangle*, Pluto Press, [1983] 1999

10. Vikram Dodd and Rory McCarthy, *Elvis Costello cancels concerts in Israel in protest at treatment of Palestinians*, Guardian, 18 May 2010

11. Salim Tamar, *A Miserable Year in Brooklyn: Khalil Sakakini in America, 1907–1908*, Jerusalem Quarterly 17, 2003, pp. 19–40

12. Gish Amit, *The Looting of the Palestinian Books*, Mitaam: A Review of Literature and Radical Thought, Vol 8, December 2006, pp. 12–22

13. Meron Benvenisti, *Sacred Landscape: the Buried History of the Holy Land since 1948*. University of California Press, 2000, p. 14

14. William Dalrymple, *A culture under fire*, Guardian, 2 October 2002

15. Jonathan Lis and Jack Khoury, *Police disperse 'Palestinian Culture Festival' events*, Haaretz, 20 March 2009

16. Asmaa Al-Ghoul, *Blockade Erodes Palestinian Culture, Education, Palestine*, Gaza Pulse, February 2013

17. Ewan MacAskill, *Israeli censors ban film about battle of Jenin*, Guardian, 12 December 2002; *Israeli Arab film-maker wins 'Jenin, Jenin' battle*, ABC News, 11 November 2003; *IDF seeks libel lawsuit against 'Jenin, Jenin' filmmakers*, MidEast Web News Service, September 26 2008; Asaf Shtull-Trauring *'Jenin, Jenin' gets Hebrew U. campus screening despite ban*, Haaretz, 16 March 2011

18. William Dalrymple, *A culture under fire*, Guardian, 2 October 2002

19. Abdelfattah Abusrour, email communication with the authors

20. Yuval Ben-Ami, *About Face*, Haaretz, 20 September 2005

21. Anshel Pfeffer, *Foreign Ministry, PR firm rebrand Israel as land of achievements*, Haaretz, 26 October 2008

22. Ethan Bronner, *After Gaza, Israel Grapples With Crisis of Isolation*, New York Times, 18 March 2009

23. Nati Tucker, *Rebranding Israel: History out, creativity and innovation*, Haaretz, 28 June 2006

24. Stephen M. Walt, *Truth and advertising*, Foreign Policy, 13 May 2009

25. Yitzhak Laor, *Putting out a contract on art*, Haaretz, 25 July 2008

26. M.Lyn Qualey, *PalFest Day 6: What is Cultural Boycott?*, Arabic Literature, 30 May 2013

27. Gideon Levy, *Puppet theatre*, Haaretz, 29 August 2010

28. Sandy Rashty, *Israeli theatre plans legal action over British Director's boycott*, Jewish Chronicle, 28 September 2012

29. *Silence is the loudest song that I can sing'*, posted on 3 January 2014 at www.marmennil.wordpress.com/2014/01/03/i-am-cancelling-my-performance-in-tel-aviv

30. *Caught in the crossfire: Should musicians boycott Israel? Al Jazeera'*, posted on 27 February 2012 at www.aljazeera.com/indepth/opinion/2012/02/20122198353750111.html

31. *Caught in the crossfire: Should musicians boycott Israel?*, posted on 27 February 2012 at www.aljazeera.com/indepth/opinion/2012/02/20122198353750111.html

32. Stephen Bates, *Ian McEwan says he will accept Jerusalem prize*, Guardian, 19 January 2011

33. Shreya Roy Chowdhury, *Amitav Ghosh lands in controversy over Israeli literary award*, The Times of India, 29 April 2010

34. *Why boycott Israeli academic institutions? Because they are complicit with the occupation of Palestine*, posted on 19 May 2009 at www.bricup.org.uk/documents/israel_unis/complicity.pdf; *Tel Aviv University to waive fees of Israeli soldiers*, posted on 26 July 2014 at www.worldbulletin.net/news/141373/tel-aviv-university-to-wave-fees-of-israeli-soldiers

35. Harriet Sherwood, *Mira Nair boycotts Haifa film festival*, the Observer, 21 July 2013

36. *Shroud Over Turin: Book Fair Boycott*, posted on 24 February 2008 at www.peoplesgeography.com/2008/02/24/shroud-over-turin

37. Walla! editorial board, *Ohad Naharin: Israelis are committing war crimes*, Occupation magazine, posted on 26 May 2005 at www.kibush.co.il/show_file.asp?num=3808; Thom Dibdin, *Anti-Israel protesters target Batsheva dance*, posted on 31 October 2012 at www.alledinburghtheatre.com/anti-israel-protesters-target-batsheva-dance

38. Naomi Wimborne-Idrissi, *BDS Batsheva Breakthrough*, posted on 8 September 2012 at www.boycottisraelnetwork.net/?p=1452

39. *Protests disrupt Proms concert by Israel Philharmonic*, posted on 2 September 2011 at www.bbc.co.uk/news/uk-14756736

40. David Fleshler, *Zubin Mehta to lead Israeli Philharmonic in Miami concert*, Miami Herald, 21 March 2014

41. Jessica Elgot, *Israel's Habima play will come to Shakespeare's Globe – thanks to the JC*, Jewish Chronicle, 19 April 2012

42. *Dismay at Globe invitation to Israeli theatre*, Guardian, 29 March 2012

43. Jessica Elgot, *London's Tricycle Theatre pulls Jewish Film Festival over Israeli Embassy funding*, The Huffington Post UK, posted on 5 August 2014 at www.huffingtonpost.co.uk/2014/08/05/tricycle-theatre-jewish-film-festival-israel_n_5651531.html; *The Guardian view on Gaza and the rise of anti-Semitism*, Guardian, 8 August 2014; Myron Jobson, *Protesters lobby the Tricycle Theatre in Kilburn over its refusal to host Jewish event*, Brent and Kilburn Times, 8 August 2014; Myron Jobson, *Investigation launched into Tricycle Theatre's £198k-a-year funding from Brent Council*, Brent and Kilburn Times, 11 August 2014; Sandy Rashty, *Culture Secretary Sajid Javid says Tricycle Theatre "misguided" over UK Jewish Film Festival boycott*, Jewish Chronicle, 12 August 2014; Martin Bright, *Muslim Tory MP: After Britain, Israel is best*, Jewish Chronicle, 13 December 2012

44. *We must stand with the Tricycle theatre*, Guardian, 15 August 2014

45. *Bristol film festival refuses Israeli Embassy funding*, posted on 29 August 2014 at www.bbc.co.uk/news/uk-england-bristol-28981867

46. Liz Lochhead, *The journey that changed my view of art and politics*, Herald, 1 September 2012

47. Omar Barghouti, speech to Palestine Solidarity Campaign AGM, posted on 21 January 2012 at www.jews4big.wordpress.com/resources-2

48. Jonathan Rosenhead, *A Mugging*, posted December 2013 at www.bricup.org.uk/documents/archive/BRICUPNewsletter71.pdf

49. Naomi Wimborne-Idrissi, *Israel is not immune to boycott*, posted on 27 April 2012 at www.opendemocracy.net/naomi-wimborne-idrissi/israel-is-not-immune-to-boycott

50. *UN Rapporteur compares Israel to Apartheid South Africa*, The Electronic Intifada, posted on 27 February 2007 at www.electronicintifada.net/content/un-rapporteur-compares-israel-apartheid-south-africa/6779

51. The Palestinian Campaign for the Academic and Cultural Boycott of Israel, revised and posted on 31 July 2014 at www.pacbi.org/etemplate.php?id=1047

52. John Smith, reply to invitation to be guest of honour at the *2014 Tel Aviv International Student Film Festival*

53. Adalah, posted at www.adalah.org/eng/Israeli-Discriminatory-Law-Database

54. Ari Shavit, *Survival of the fittest*, Haaretz, 8 January 2004

55. *Settler violence and encroachment*, United Nations Office for the Coordination of Humanitarian Affairs Annual Report, posted at www.ochaopt.org/annual/c2/6.html

56. *Human Rights in Palestine and other: Report of the United Nations Fact-Finding Mission on the Gaza*, posted at www2.ohchr.org/english/bodies/hrcouncil/docs/12session/A-HRC-12-48.pdf

57. Etgar Lefkovits, *Leaders pledge to end arms smuggling*, Jerusalem Post, 18 January 2009

58. Rafael Ahren, *Solana: EU has closer ties to Israel than potential member Croatia*, Haaretz, 21 October 2009

59. Jewish Virtual Library posted at www.jewishvirtuallibrary.org/jsource/UN/usvetoes.html; United Nations Dag Hammarskjöld Library Research Guide, posted at www.research.un.org/en/docs/sc/quick/veto

Published by Artists for Palestine UK
Co-authored by a collective of artists and activists © 2015
ISBN: 978-0-9931767-0-8

For further information, or to order copies, see:
www.artistsforpalestine.org.uk

Contact:
artistsforpalestine@gmail.com

Design:
Fraser Muggeridge studio

Acknowledgements:
With thanks to Kamila Shamsie. Shamsie is a novelist, reviewer and columnist whose work has been translated into over 20 languages.